THE YOUNG INVESTORS ROADMAP TO SUCCESS

BRETT AUBREY GORDON

ARCHWAY
PUBLISHING

Archway Publishing books may be ordered through booksellers or by contacting:

Archway Publishing
1663 Liberty Drive
Bloomington, IN 47403
www.archwaypublishing.com
844-669-3957

Because of the dynamic nature of the Internet, any web addresses or
links contained in this book may have changed since publication and
may no longer be valid. The views expressed in this work are solely those
of the author and do not necessarily reflect the views of the publisher,
and the publisher hereby disclaims any responsibility for them.

Any people depicted in stock imagery provided by Getty Images are
models, and such images are being used for illustrative purposes only.
Certain stock imagery © Getty Images.

ISBN: 978-1-6657-2132-5 (sc)
ISBN: 978-1-6657-2133-2 (e)

Library of Congress Control Number: 2022906104

Print information available on the last page.

Archway Publishing rev. date: 04/06/2022

CONTENTS

THE INVESTMENT MINDSET

Have you ever wondered why most of the wealthiest people have their wealth tied up in investments like company stocks and real estate?

Well, the reason is simple! These are the tools that rich people have used to become rich in the first place.

ACHIEVING THE INVESTMENT MINDSET

Not every person understands the value of acquiring an investor mindset. By this, I simply mean that not everyone realizes the importance of making investments. Given a choice, many people will choose to gratify their current desires, like buying a car or buying a new watch, rather than saving up and investing that money for later.

Why do people make this choice? Don't they know what is good or bad for them?

The problem is that we live in a society now that is more connected because of social media than it used to be a few decades back. You are constantly bombarded with other people's "lavish" lifestyles—flying in private jets, partying on private yachts, and, in general, living an extravagant life.

It is no wonder that you start to feel that you are missing out on the "good things" in life, and you start to spend every dollar you earn trying to replicate that picturesque life for yourself rather than invest in building a stable future for your family.

The one other thing that I blame for people not developing an investor's mindset is our education system. Our schools and colleges have failed to teach children how to manage their finances. You will not find any school inculcating the habit of saving and investing in their students or teaching them about personal finances/investments.

These are habits that, if not developed at an early age, are very hard to adopt later in life. Not every child is fortunate enough to have financially savvy parents who can teach them this at an early age, and so the responsibility really lies on our education system.

The irony of the whole situation is that not only do they not teach you this stuff at school but many students actually take on huge amounts of debt just to even attend a university. By the time they graduate, they are neck deep in debt, which they then have to pay off by working a nine-to-five job.

How are they going to invest if they cannot save?

This is one of the things that separates the rich from the poor. The poor work for a living, whereas the rich make their money work for them.

Let me explain how!

When you work in a job, you are essentially selling your working hours to your employer.

Some people might have more valuable skills than others, which is why they are able to extract a better compensation for their working hours and charge their employer a higher rate. Some people might not be that fortunate and might be working at minimum wage. But in both scenarios the workers are still selling their time.

How much of your time can you sell? Nine hours a day? Twelve hours a day?

And for how long do you think you can work a nine- to-five job?

An average 20-year-old might be able to work productively for more than 12 hours a day. An average 50-year-old can work no more than 8 hours productively in a day. An average 60-year-old can work no more than 6 hours productively each day. This situation keeps getting worse with age.

This is what we call human capital, and the graph below shows how it decreases with age.

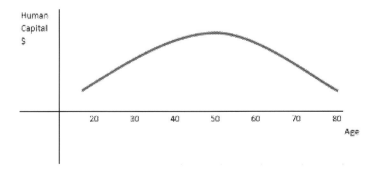

It is around the age-50 mark that your human capital starts to decrease. If you have not been saving for all these years, then you will find yourself in a tough spot. This is how the poor approach the notion of creating wealth, and as you can see from the graph above, the odds are stacked against them. They are playing a losing game.

The only way out of the rat race and to have a real chance at creating wealth is to start saving and investing at a very young age. This way, by the time you reach the age of 50 and your human capital starts to decline, the returns on your investment portfolio will be more than enough to balance it out.

This is how the rich have historically played the game. The rich make their money work for them. They learn at a very young age about the power of compounding.

THE POWER OF COMPOUNDING

In simple language, compounding is when you earn profit on both the amount you have saved and the profit you have earned until now.

For example, let us say you have $100, and you earn 10% on it for year 1 and year 2. The profit in year 1 would be $10, whereas the profit in year 2 would be $11. Although the percentage profit is constant at 10%, the dollar amount of the profit has increased from $10 to $11 between the two years. This is called the compounding effect, and it exponentially increases the value of an investment portfolio.

Let me tell you a very old story of a king and one of his countrymen.

There was once a very powerful king ruling over a very vast piece of land. His riches and wealth seemed to have no bounds. This king enjoyed playing games, and after playing every kind of game that was available at that time, he challenged his countrymen to invent a new game that would impress him.

After a few weeks had passed by, a man came to the palace and asked to show the king a newly invented game. This game was called chess, and it was a strategy- based game. The king was so impressed by the new game that he said to the man, "Name your reward."

The man thought for a moment and then responded, "Oh, sire, my wishes are simple. I only wish for this. If you place just one grain of rice on the first square of the chessboard and double it for every subsequent square, I will consider myself well rewarded."

The king was reluctant at first, as he wanted to give the man a much bigger reward for his invention, perhaps in the form of gold. But eventually he agreed to give the man what he had asked for. Upon the king's order, the royal treasurer started to calculate the amount of rice that needed to be given to the inventor.

The treasurer placed one grain of rice on the first square, two on the second square, four on the third square, and so on. By the time he reached the 10th square, he had to place 512 grains of rice. On the 20th square, the number swelled up to 524,288 grains of rice. Halfway through the chessboard, the number had reached 2,147,483,648 or approximately 2.15 billion grains of rice. When the treasurer reached the last square on the chessboard, he realized that the king owed around 9,223,372,036,854,780,000 or 9.2 quintillion grains of rice to the inventor. The figure was so huge that eventually the king, to honor his word, had to leave his throne and give it to this wise man.

This is how compounding works. If you learn to harness the power compounding, you will achieve financial freedom very early in your lifetime. This book will teach you all about compounding and how to achieve it through value investing.

BE AN INVESTOR, NOT A SPECULATOR

The terms speculator and investor are usually incorrectly used interchangeably in the market. Some people might call themselves investors, but they are doing nothing more than placing bets in the financial markets. These are actually the speculators.

Speculating involves putting your money at risk in the hope of earning a profit in the very short run. Day-trading, where stock trades are opened and closed in hours, is a good example of speculating. Speculators take on a very high level of risk in the hope of a big reward. However, with such a high level of risk, they can also experience huge losses and lose their capital as well.

Investing, on the other hand, is done for the long term. An investor does not buy the stock just because he or she can make a quick gain from it and sell it in a few minutes' time.

When an investor buys a stock, he is buying an ownership stake in the business. As an owner, he is also eligible for any dividends that the company announces after it makes a profit in every quarter.

Warren Buffett once famously said, "I buy on the assumption that they could close the market the next day and not reopen it for five years." This shows you that Warren Buffett is a long-term investor, and he is not fazed at all by the daily noise in the financial markets.

So how do long-term investors decide which stock to buy?

Although we will cover this in more detail in the next few chapters, the basic principle behind value investing is to conduct comprehensive fundamental analysis of a company's financial statements and figure out what it is currently worth. We also call this finding out the intrinsic value.

If the company is overvalued, which means that its intrinsic value is less than what it is currently trading for in the market, then the investor should not invest in it.

If the company is undervalued, which means that its intrinsic value is higher than what it is currently trading for in the market, then the investor should buy the company stock.

Benjamin Graham and David Dodd, founders of value investing, coined the term margin of safety.

If a company stock is currently trading for $80 in the market, and you calculate its intrinsic value to be around $83, then there is not enough margin of safety for you to invest in the stock.

On the other hand, if a company stock is currently trading for $80 in the market, but you calculate its value to be around $120, then there is enough margin of safety for you to proceed with the investment.

Another key ingredient to successful value investing is to ensure that the company you invest in has good management and strategic vision. Additionally, it should have a consistent dividend-paying history.

Warren Buffett really loves to invest in dividend-paying company stocks, as it helps him to harness the power of compounding each year. The dividends he receives from his existing investments are reinvested in more undervalued companies to make him more dividends the next year. This cycle has been going on for more than sixty years. That is why he is now worth billions of dollars.

Diversification is also a key characteristic of a balanced investment. The more company stocks you have in your portfolio (from various sectors and industries), the higher the diversification benefit that you will achieve. Greater diversification significantly reduces the risk in your investment portfolio. Avoiding a huge loss is one of the bedrocks on which the foundation of value investing is laid. The greatest value investors called this preservation of capital.

THE INVESTMENT UNIVERSE

Stocks/equity is not the only thing that you can invest in. There are plenty of other investments that you can choose.

1. Fixed-Income Securities

Investing in stocks/equity is not everyone's cup of tea. Not everyone is willing to take the risks that stocks expose you to.

What do I mean by risk?

Well, risk basically means not knowing what will happen to your investment. Will it gain value or lose value in the future?

How do you know if you are a risk-taker or a risk-avoider? Let me ask you a simple question. If you had the following two choices to make, which one would you go for?

- Choice 1: Flip a coin. If it is heads, you get $1,000. If it is tails, you get $0.
- Choice 2: Receive a fixed amount of $100 irrespective of whether it is heads or tails.

If you chose the first option, that means you are a risk-taker, and you are not afraid to put money at risk for the potential of a bigger reward.

If, on the other hand, you chose to go with option two, that means you like to play it safe. "A bird in the hand is better than two in the bush" is the kind of philosophy that you go by.

Do not get me wrong. Neither option is good or bad! The amount of risk an individual can take will differ from person to person.

Some people would prefer to have a stable and predictable fixed return.

So how do fixed-income securities work exactly, you ask?

Fixed-income securities are debt instruments that pay a fixed rate of interest to the investor based on the investment structure over a period of time. At maturity, the investor is also repaid the original investment amount.

Like I have mentioned before, fixed-income securities offer a more predictable income for investors. But since they are generally safer investments, their returns are lower than that of equities in the long run.

Investment is all about a risk/return trade-off. The higher the risk you take, the higher your potential returns could be. The lower the risk you take, the lower your potential returns will be.

Some examples of fixed-income instruments are Treasury bills, Treasury bonds, corporate bonds, and term finance certificates.

2. Mutual Funds

There are some people who like to be actively involved in the decision-making of their investments, whether it be in stocks, fixed income, or any other asset, for that matter. They do not mind the hours or even days of extensive research they must conduct before making up their mind on which stocks to buy.

And then there are others like my dear, old father.

My dad used to love investing in mutual funds. He used to tell me, "Son, why do something yourself when you can get an expert, who can do a better job, to do it for you?"

That is why individuals who are not experts in the field turn to mutual funds as an alternative.

A mutual fund pools the savings of several investors and in return gives them "units" that represent their share of the total investment, and then dividends/capital gains are realized based on these units.

Investing in mutual funds is very simple—so simple that even a blindfolded monkey can do it.

Mutual funds can be of two types:

   i)   Open ended: An open-ended fund is one in which you buy directly from the mutual fund company. It is available for subscription all through the year. These do not have a fixed maturity.

Investors can conveniently buy and sell units at closing-day net asset value (NAV) prices. The main advantage of these funds is their liquidity. You can redeem your funds at any time without worrying too much about the overall liquidity situation in the stock exchange.

ii) Close ended: A close-end fund is offered to the public in an initial public offering (IPO). Once the units are issued, they can be bought or sold through the stock exchange just like shares. Their liquidity depends on how liquid the stock market is on a particular day. The benefit you get from investing in a mutual fund is that experienced managers are managing your capital in return for a management fee, usually ranging from anywhere between 1 and 3% of your total investment value. These investment managers are experts in their field, and they always have their finger on the pulse of the economy. Therefore, these professionals can claim to do a better job at managing your funds than you can.

You can select from hundreds and thousands of mutual funds offering their services by evaluating their historical performance. Go for the one that has the most consistent performance!

Mutual funds can be of various types. There are equity funds, fixed-income funds, money-market funds (short-term debt funds), and balanced funds, to name a few. Selecting the type of fund really depends on your risk appetite. If you want to go for high risk, you can select an aggressive equity fund. If you want more regular income, you can select a money-market fund or a fixed-income fund. On the other hand, if you want a diversified portfolio containing both equities and fixed income, you can select balanced funds. You have a lot of options. If you are confused about which fund you should invest in, then you should approach a financial advisor, who will assess your risk profile and recommend a suitable option.

Besides professional management, another benefit of investing in a mutual fund is that you get an exposure to a diversified portfolio even with a small investment amount. For instance, if you have $1,000 and opt to invest directly in the market, you will not be able to have an exposure to more than 2 or 3 companies at a time. But in a mutual fund, even with a $1,000 investment, you will have an exposure to around 30 or more companies at a time. This is because in a mutual fund, you are given "units" of a collective investment pool that has invested in various companies across multiple sectors.

If mutual funds are so attractive and easy to invest in, why do people still invest directly in the stock market?

Although there are many benefits to investing in mutual funds, there are always two sides to a coin!

One of the problems with mutual funds is that you will not have direct control over how your funds are being managed. You will not know the exact composition of stocks in your portfolio at any given point in time. Nor will you be able to influence the stocks that your fund manager buys in the portfolio.

Another big disadvantage of owning mutual funds is that their expense ratios are too high. They not only charge you a certain management fee for looking after your portfolio but there are many hidden and implicit costs as well. These include brokerage fees, spillage costs and delay costs, et cetera.

Spillage cost occurs when a trade is executed at a price different than the one that was expected/requested. Delay cost represents the loss in investment value between the time a manager makes the decision to buy a certain stock and the time the order is released into the market.

All these explicit and implicit costs have a large drag on the returns in the long run. Most value investors like Warren Buffett and Charlie Munger really dislike mutual funds for this very reason.

3. Market Index funds

In 2016, Warren Buffett famously wrote in a letter to his shareholders that "when trillions of dollars are managed by Wall Streeters charging high fees, it will usually be the managers who reap outsized profits, not the clients. Both large and small investors should stick with low-cost index funds."

If you do not want to pay these high costs associated with the actively managed mutual funds either, you should invest in a market index fund too.

What are index funds, you ask?

An index fund is a form of mutual fund whose holdings track a particular index of the market, like the Dow Jones Industrial Average or the S&P 500. This type of investing is also commonly referred to as "passive investing" because it is more of a hands-off approach.

All the fund manager is doing is creating a portfolio that fully or partially replicates the performance of a particular index. Expenses are lower for index funds because there are no management fees as compared to a traditional mutual fund. These lower costs can make a significant difference in your returns over the long run.

One of the advantages of investing in a market index fund is that it is super tax efficient. By trading less frequently as compared to an actively managed mutual fund, index funds generate lower taxable income that is passed to their shareholders.

Index funds have another tax advantage as well. Since index funds buy lots of new securities each time a new investor puts money into the fund, they may have thousands of lots to choose from when selling a particular security. That means they can choose the one that will produce the lowest capital gains and, therefore, the lowest tax bite.

Market index funds are the best investment vehicle for a conservative investor who wants to save on as much management costs as possible.

The major drawback with index funds is that they are highly correlated to the returns of the index. This means that the portfolio value will increase as the index rises, and the portfolio value will decline as the index falls. During a financial crisis, you will be completely exposed to a falling index, whereas an actively managed mutual fund manager might sense early that trouble is looming and adjust the portfolio positions accordingly.

Another problem with a market index fund is that it is overdiversified. This means that it will usually have more holdings than an actively managed mutual fund. The broad-based index might not do well due to certain underperformers that will lower your returns as compared to the more "cherry-picked" portfolio of an active mutual fund manager.

4. Exchange-Traded Funds (ETFs)

Exchange-traded funds are similar to market index funds, as they too track a particular index. The only difference is that they trade on the stock exchange. You can buy and sell ETFs at any time during the day based on ask/bid quotes. In contrast, market index funds can be bought and sold only at the day-end closing prices.

Just like index funds, ETFs are well diversified and less costly. They have tax advantages over mutual funds because capital gains tax on an ETF is only incurred if an investor chooses to sell his ETFs.

One unique disadvantage of an ETF is that since it is traded on the stock exchange, investors might fall into the trap of overtrading. Not all investors act rationally when they are in the market. Many more investors trade based on their emotions rather than logic. This is when overtrading happens. After a few initial successful trades, an investor becomes overconfident in their ability to accurately predict the market. Next thing you know, they start to use leverage in their trades. In no time, they make a wrong move and lose their entire capital.

WHICH INVESTMENT VEHICLE TO CHOOSE

The investment vehicles that I have described above are not your only investment opportunities. There are many more, and with time there will be new investment products created as well. Other investment vehicles include retire- ment accounts such as 401(k) plans and IRA or deriva- tive contracts, including future contracts, option contracts, and collateralized debt obligations (CDOs), just to name a few.

Which investment vehicle you choose will depend on what your goals are and how much risk you can take. Meet a financial advisor, and discuss your financial situation with them. Work together to draw up an investor policy statement (IPS) for yourself.

This is a good first step in identifying what you want from an investment. Based on this IPS, you can then go on to evaluating the different investment opportunities and choosing the one that best serves your financial needs.

BUYING A BUSINESS

I remember on my ninth birthday, my dad bought me a hundred shares of The Coca-Cola Company as a birthday gift. Back then, the shares used to be physical paper certificates you could hold in your hands. Nowadays they are mostly digital and just numbers in your trading accounts.

I took the physical shares that my dad gave me and stared at them blankly for about a minute. I had no clue what this piece of paper meant. Was it some sort of ticket to Disneyland or some other adventure place? As I investigated it further, I saw the words The Coca-Cola Company written in block letters on the front.

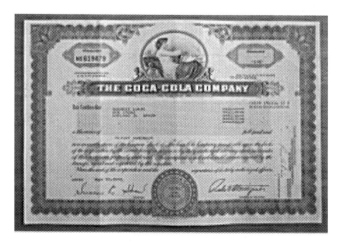

It made me wonder—was this the same company that sold those Coke bottles I drank almost every day during my recess time at school?

Was Dad planning to take me to see a Coca-Cola Company factory?

After keeping me in suspense for what seemed to be an excruciatingly long time, my dad broke his silence by saying, "Son, how does it feel to be a proud co-owner of The Coca-Cola Company?"

I did not know what to make of this piece of information at the time. I was still a young kid and had absolutely no idea about business. So I asked him, "Dad, what is a co-owner, and does that mean I can visit the factory?"

He chuckled and replied, "Son, with these hundred shares of Coca-Cola, you now own a part of the fizzy- drinks company. You have thousands of employees working for you and have factories across the world. You can attend the annual general meetings of the company and even vote on important decisions they make. Every three months, the company will send you an annual report that will tell you how much profit the company has made for that quarter. If the company makes a profit, they can even announce a dividend. Since you are now the shareholder of a hundred shares, you will also get a certain portion of these dividends as well."

He continued, "Isn't that just great? Not only that but if your company is consistently doing well quarter over quarter, the stock price of the company will also rise, and your hundred shares will be worth a lot more than they are today."

I remember that night I felt over the moon about owning my very first business. I could not sleep the entire night because I was too anxious to tell my friends all about it the next morning in school.

Sure enough, my friends were fascinated, and they even asked me if I could now give them a friends-and-family discount on the Coke bottles that they were going to buy.

I told them that I would think about it!

CHAPTER 2

BUYING THE BUSINESS, NOT STOCKS

THOUGH I DIDN'T KNOW IT at the time, my dad taught me one of the greatest lessons in value investing that day.

Investing is about having ownership in your business. A business owner has a long-term perspective, and he is not worried about the short-term price volatility in the stock market. This is because he does not intend to sell his shares right now. He is in it for the long haul and is waiting for the company to expand and achieve its vision. He knows that once the company reaches that stage, he can cash out his shares at a much higher price then, if he wants to. One of the world's most successful value investors, Warren Buffett, once said, "I never attempt to make money on the stock market. I buy on the assumption that they could close the market the next day and not reopen it for five years."

This is contrary to what many Wall Street traders find themselves doing day in and day out. They like to take daily positions and exit these before the market closes in order to make a quick buck or two.

A casino player making bets on the poker table or playing the slot machines is no different. Both the trader and the casino player have their strategies and tactics that they claim work for them. These might even work for the first few gambles—call it beginner's luck. But in the long run, the house always wins.

Warren Buffett summed this up beautifully by saying, "The stock market is a device for transferring money from the impatient to the patient."

This is a very important lesson for all young investors out there. The greatest asset you have is time. If you start investing from a very young age, over time your investment amount will grow exponentially due to a phenomenon called the compounding effect, which I told you about in greater detail earlier.

The question now remains how to know which businesses to invest in and which ones to stay away from.

FIND WELL-MANAGED COMPANIES

There are two lemonade stands on the street selling the same-tasting lemonade. One of them is run by a kid named George, who is rude to his customers and does not care about any of the other things like cleanliness or even the packaging of the drink. The other lemonade stand is run by Michael, who has always loved being a people person and runs his stall very efficiently too. He makes small talk with all his customers and greets them well. He is very attentive to the finer details, like maintaining cleanliness in his stall, recording all his sales and expenses in his diary, and improving the packaging of his lemonade drink. He is even planning to expand his business by building a second counter and asking his cousin Mary to handle that.

All things considered, if I gave you the option of buying either Michael's stall or George's stall, which one would you choose?

Naturally, you would think the chances of success for Michael's stall are far better, and so you should invest in that. The same basic principle also applies when deciding to invest in much bigger public limited companies.

Management can make a huge difference in the success of a company. Good management can add a lot of value beyond a company's hard assets, while on the other hand, bad management can bring even the most financially strong companies to absolute ruin.

In fact, choosing the company with the right management is so important that many successful value investors base their entire investing strategy on finding managers who are the most capable and ethical.

Warren Buffett identifies three key qualities that you should look for in the management of the company you are planning to invest in: integrity, intelligence, and energy. He adds that "if they don't have the first, the other two will kill you."

A good way to test the integrity of the management is by going through the company's annual reports. You will get a good sense of the management's honesty. How well have they fulfilled their past promises? How have they tackled any negative press against them? Have they taken responsibility for any failed ventures, or have they blamed it on other external circumstances?

One conflict of interest that usually happens between management and the owners/shareholders of the company is that managers might have short-term goals that are not in line with creating long-term value for the owners. For example, managers might invest more in short-term projects that temporarily inflate the company's earnings to justify higher bonuses and compensations for them. The size and reporting of compensation are usually one of the biggest giveaways of a conflict of interest.

These are some of the things that you should be on the lookout for when investing in a business. You want to have management with the highest level of integrity. This is why Warren Buffett invests in companies with really good management. If the management of a company is not up to his standards, he goes on to buy a majority shareholding (51%) of the company and votes his own management in to take things over.

FINDING THE INTRINSIC VALUE OF A BUSINESS

If you are looking for the next big thing, a company that might be great in time, then you cannot really call yourself an investor. In the eyes of Benjamin Graham, the father of value investing, you are just a speculator if you are doing that. An investor does not put his money in something that might work out well in the future.

On the contrary, value investors are on the lookout for bargain deals and once-in-a-lifetime value purchases. Sometimes, markets tend to overreact to negative news about a company, and the price of their stock falls way lower than what it is worth. These deep discounts to the intrinsic value of a company are a prime buying opportunity for value investors. Call it a flash sale, if you will, where you can buy good companies for discounts sometimes as high as 75%.

But how do you determine if something is selling at a discounted price or not?

For that you would first need to know the intrinsic value of a company. Intrinsic value is nothing more than a fancy way of saying how much your company is worth. There are many ways you can go about valuing a company, most of which we will cover later in the book.

Perhaps one of the simplest ways is through a company's price-to-earning ratio, or P/E ratio. It is the ratio of the company's stock price to its earnings per share.

Earnings per share can be thought of as the total leftover profits of a company after it has paid for all its costs, expenses, and taxes, divided by the total number of shares the company has issued so far.

Price to Earnings Ratio = Company Stock Price

Earnings Per Share

Think of P/E as the earning power of a company— how many years it takes to cover the price if earnings stay the same.

Let me give you a simple example:

Company A is a cement-manufacturing company. Its share price is $36 per share, and the earnings per share in the last fiscal year were $6 per share. This means that the P/E ratio will be six times or that it will take six years for the company's earnings to cover the stock price assuming earnings remain constant.

Similarly, Company B is also a cement-manufacturing company and is a competitor of Company A. The share price of Company B is $64 per share, and the earnings per share are $8. This means that its P/E ratio is eight times or that it will take eight years for the company's earnings to cover the stock's price.

At first glance, you may think that Company B is a better investment because it is giving you higher earnings per share. But what you need to also consider is that you are paying twice as much for Company B's stock price as well. This means if you have a total investment of only $64, you will be able to buy only one stock of Company B, producing $8 per share, or two stocks of Company A, producing a total of $12 for both shares. Your return on investment is higher if you invest in Company A.

You should be able to conclude that Company A is relatively undervalued as compared to Company B and better for investment, assuming all other factors are held constant.

Alternatively, you can use the P/E ratio directly to conclude which company you should invest in or which is relatively cheaper to buy. This is called relative valuation. You will basically come to the same conclusion.

Company A has a P/E ratio of six, while Company B ratio has a P/E of eight. A lower P/E ratio is better, since it indicates you are paying less per dollar of earnings of the company. Thus, Company A comes out to be the winner in this valuation exercise as well.

You can change the metric to suit your analysis. For some industries, the price-to-earnings ratio will be a good ratio to use. For other industries, you might want to use price-to-sales ratio or price-to-cash flow ratio. The basic principle in making the comparative investment decision will remain the same whichever price-multiple ratio you end up using.

INVESTING GUIDELINES

When it comes to investing in or buying a business, using just one simple P/E ratio is simply not enough. There are many other elements of the financial position of the company that you must consider. Some of them are given below.

1.   Price/Earnings-to-Growth (PEG) ratio

For instance, it could very well be a fact that a company is trading at a lower P/E ratio than its competitor not because it is mispriced by the market but rather because it is experiencing falling growth rate. This means that its revenues/profits are expected to further decline in the future. Investing in such a company is actually called a value trap because it may seem that it is selling for a discounted price, but it actually isn't, because its earning per share and subsequently price-to-earnings ratio are expected to fall even more.

Therefore, investing in stable and growing companies is more preferable for the average investor.

How do we factor this growth element into the P/E ratio, you ask?

Well, we just adjust the P/E ratio by dividing it by the growth factors of the company.

Let us continue with our previous example.

We saw that Company A was a better investment choice based on the earlier information given as compared to Company B. Now let me tell you that Company A is growing at only 2%, while company B is growing at 8% annually.

This changes the whole dynamics of the situation. The PEG ratio for Company A will be equal to:

P/E ratio of Company A

Earnings growth rate of Company = 6 times divided by 2%

This will give us a PEG ratio of three times for Company A. If we do a similar calculation for Company B (8 times divided by 8%), we will get a PEG ratio of 1 time for Company B.

After incorporating growth rate of the respective companies in our formula, we can now conclude that Company B has the lower and therefore better PEG ratio— making it a better investment.

2.   Debt-to-Equity (D/E) Ratio

Another thing to look for to determine a company's financial stability is its debt-to-equity ratio.

A company's debt-to-equity ratio is found by dividing its total liabilities by its owner's equity. In simple words, it tells us how much of the company is run from debt or other people's money. The more debt a company has, the more interest it has to pay. In good times, company profits will be more than enough to cover debt principal and interest payments. However, it is the bad times that we need to worry about. If the economy is in a recession and the company is not making much in sales, how will it pay off its debt obligations? Debt financing opens the business to risk because of this. As we saw earlier, value investors are not speculators, and they don't like to invest in highly debt-financed companies. We also call these companies highly leveraged.

Therefore, value investors look to invest in companies that preferably have a debt-to-equity ratio of less than one.

3.   Price-to-Book (P/B) Ratio

This ratio is found by dividing a company's stock price by its shares book value. It basically tells you what the market is valuing the company compared to the company's value in its own books—assets minus liabilities.

As you know by now, value investors like to buy companies at a discount to the intrinsic value. That means a company with a price-to-book value of less than one will be considered a bargain.

A CONTRARIAN APPROACH TO INVESTING

You can use any of the valuation tools above to assess which company is the cheapest to invest in. This often means that you have to find that one "golden" stock among a thousand others—a diamond in the rough. It might have been completely ignored by others or just has not received much coverage or spotlight in the media.

This is why value investing is often termed as a contrarian approach to investing. Speculators, on the other hand, follow the herd, which is called herd investing. When a company stock is in the news a lot and has already spiked significantly in price, this is when the speculators jump in and buy that stock in the anticipation that it will go even higher. This is a deadly mistake!

They usually get stuck buying very expensive stocks, which don't perform (financially) nearly as well as they were expected to. Thus, speculators keep on making such bets and keep losing their money. They lack a disciplined approach. But value investors seek to minimize such losses by following a disciplined approach of buying stocks at a discounted price and waiting for the market to accurately price them again.

IGNORE THE MARKET 99% OF THE TIME

The central theme for value investors has and always will be to treat company stocks as businesses they love and want to see grow. The value investor is in it for the long haul, and he is not afraid of the short-term adverse price movements of his investments in the market.

Haven't you heard before on the news that Elon Musk, Bill Gates, or Jeff Bezos lost billions of dollars in a single day because of a market correction in the stock market?

Are these billionaires at all worried? The answer is no. They don't even look at the market that often. That is because they have no intention to sell their investments.

The market only matters when you enter or exit a position. The rest of the time it should be completely ignored.

CHAPTER 3

DECODING THE FINANCIALS

My dad made it a point to teach me and my brother about personal finance, wealth, and investments from a very early age. He belonged to the school of thought that believed that if financial habits are not developed at a young age, it is really hard to do so when you get older.

I even remember him jokingly tell someone in a dinner party once, "If you want to teach your children about taxes, eat 30% of their ice cream." Obviously, it goes without saying he never did that with us. Maybe he should have!

He taught me and my brother the value of earning and saving for ourselves. At the age of ten, I asked my dad to buy me the new Nintendo gaming console. It was all the craze back then, and all my friends at school had one. I confronted my dad about it and told him that I needed one as well. After all, I didn't want to be the only kid at school who didn't have a Nintendo. In all honesty, this was the first time I had ever asked my dad for something expensive.

Unlike a typical dad, who would just go out and get the Nintendo for his kid as an early Christmas gift or something, he asked me to accompany him to our neighbor's house to meet with Bob Vance. He told Bob that I wanted to buy a Nintendo for myself and asked him whether I could help around his yard for an hourly wage. Bob was more than happy to let me work on his backyard, as he was busy with his business lately and just could not find the time to tend to his yard himself.

For the next couple of months, I worked for Bob Vance—mowing his lawn, adding fresh flowers to his flower beds, trimming the hedges, painting the fence, taking out the weeds, and so on.

I got to know more about Bob's business by talking to him about it from time to time. He was a nice fellow and never really got irritated by any of my inquisitive and sometimes even very personal questions. Bob told me that he had started a donut shop a few years back after quitting his nine-to-five job. He had come a long way since then and now was operating a full-scale business with good sales and profit numbers.

One day, when I went to his house to ask for some garden tools, he was sitting in his study reviewing some documents related to his business. It was always intriguing to me to get to know more about his business, and so I asked him what he was working on.

Bob, being the patient soul that he was, noticed that I was keen on learning some business skills from him. He invited me to join him and handed me a few documents to look at. They turned out to be the financial statements for his company for the last quarter. That day we spent almost three hours in his study as he explained to me each and every major component of his financial statements.

I think he loved teaching it to me as much as I loved learning it from him. We had so much fun discussing business that we both lost track of time, and eventually my dad knocked on Bob's front door to tell us it was getting late and that I had to go to sleep to get up early for school the next morning.

FINANCIAL STATEMENTS

For those of you who don't know what financial statements are, you can simply think of them as business reports that depict the financial situation/health of a company. This is why it is important to review the financial statements of a company before you decide to invest in it, because you don't want to end up in a situation where you invest in a loss-making company.

Bob told me that there are two groups of people who use the financial statements: internal users and external users. Internal users include people like the management of the company or the board of directors. Bob, CEO of the donut shop, counted as an internal user, and so did his wife, who was part of the board of directors as well.

External users include investors and creditors, meaning people outside of the company who have no other source of financial information about the company except for the published financial reports. Investors want to know how profitable a company is and whether it will grow in the future. On the other hand, creditors aren't as concerned with the profitability of the company as investors are. They are more concerned with the cash flows of the company and whether the company generates enough to pay back the loans.

There are three important financial statements: income statement, balance sheet, and statement of cash flows.

THE INCOME STATEMENT

Bob told me that the income statement is also called a profit-and-loss account. This report basically tells Bob how much profit/loss his donut shop makes during a specific period of time. It shows a summary of all his income, expenses, and the resulting profit/loss during a period. Management also typically prepares departmental statements that break revenue and expense numbers down by different business segments. However, Bob's income statement was not that complex at the moment.

The period for which these statements are prepared can vary from company to company. Larger, publicly listed companies release their financial reports every quarter, whereas some smaller private companies might do it on a more frequent basis, such as monthly.

There are two income statement formats you could use while preparing it:

1. Single-step income statement

This is a simpler way of preparing an income statement. It shows only one category of income and one category of expenses. It is less useful for external users because they may not be able to calculate many profitability or efficiency ratios with this limited data. Below is an example of what the single-step income statement typically looks like:

Income Statement - Single Step For the Quarter ended December 31, 1975	$	$
Revenues:		
Food Sales	248,000	
Souvenir Sales	30,000	
Total Revenues		278,000
Expenses:		
Cost of Goods Sold	102,000	
Depreciation Expense	20,000	
Wage Expense	7,500	
Rent Expense	5,000	
Interest Expense	5,000	
Supplies Expense	5,000	
Utilities Expense	4,000	
Total Expenses		148,500
Net Income		129,500

Step 2: If you are selling a product, let us say a pack of donuts, you will directly incur some costs related to its manufacturing process. For donuts, this will include things like the cost of the ingredients used and the cost of packaging. These costs are referred to as "cost of goods sold." One way of calculating the cost of goods sold is through the following formula:

Cost of goods sold = Beginning inventory

+ Purchases – Ending inventory

Step 3: The next step in preparing an income statement is calculating the gross profit. It can be calculated using the following formula:

Gross profit = Sales − Cost of goods sold Therefore, gross profit is the profit that the company makes before deducting any other expenses related to manufacturing or selling of the product.

Step 4: Next come the operating expenses of a business. These are usually categorized into selling, general, and administrative (SG&A) expenses.

 i) Selling expenses can include advertising expenses or sales commissions.
 ii) General and administrative expenses can include rent expense, utilities, supplies, et cetera.

Step 5: If you deduct the operating expenses from the gross profit, you arrive at the income from operations.

Income from operations = Gross profit − operating expenses

Step 6: Nonoperating income and expenses are calculated in this step. These do not relate directly to the core operations of the company. They might include things like insurance proceeds and interest expenses.

Step 7: Net income is then calculated by deducting the nonoperating income/expenses from the "income from operations."

Net income = Income from operations − Nonoperating income and expenses

BALANCE SHEET

The next financial statement that Bob showed me was his balance sheet. He told me that a balance sheet shows the financial position of a company and provides a snapshot of a company's assets, liabilities, and equity at a given moment in time.

The balance sheet is basically a report version of the accounting equation where assets must always equal liabilities plus equity. There is a simple way of understanding this equation if you have not come across this before:

Assets = Liabilities + Equity

Let us suppose you want to buy a piece of land. Your assets will increase, since land is considered an asset because it provides an economic value to you. Now, to finance the purchase of the asset, you can either borrow the money from someone (also called liabilities) or use your own money (called equity). The process by which both of these transactions are recorded in the financial statements is called the "double-entry bookkeeping" system, and the balance sheet is a simple visual representation of the accounting equation.

Bob's balance sheet looked like this:

	$	$
Bob Vance Donuts Inc.		
Balance Sheet		
As of December 31, 1975		
Assets		
Current Assets		
Cash		328,000
Accounts Receivable		3,000
Prepaid Rent		10,000
Inventory		398,000
Total Current Assets		739,000
Fixed Assets		
Equipment	200,000	
Vehicles	100,000	
Land and Building	700,000	
Accumulated Depreciation	20,000	980,000
Total Assets		**1,719,000**
Liabilities		
Current Liabilities		
Accounts Payable		490,000
Accrued Expenses		4,500
Unearned Revenue		10,000
Total Current Liabilities		504,500
Long Term Liabilities		995,000
		1,499,500
Equity		
Owners Equity		
Retained Earnings		119,500
Common Stock		100,000
Total Owner's Equity		219,500
Total Liabilities and Owner's Equity		**1,719,000**

On the asset side of Bob's balance sheet, there were both current assets and fixed assets. Current assets are all those assets of a company that are expected to be sold or used as a result of standard business operations over the next year.

These include:

I) Cash at Bank: since the cash in your bank is a highly liquid asset and can be withdrawn at any moment in time, it is treated as a current asset.

II) Accounts Receivable: when people owe you money that they need to pay within a year, this amount goes into the accounts receivable category.

III) Inventory: for Bob's donuts, this includes the ingredients for the donuts as well as the ready- for-sale donuts.

Fixed assets, on the other hand, are long-term assets that a company has purchased and is using for the production of its goods and services. For Bob's donut shop, his fixed assets included his donut-making equipment, his delivery trucks/vehicles, and his land and building.

Total assets are simply the sum of all current assets and fixed assets.

On the other side of the balance sheet, we have liabilities and equity. Liabilities are also of two types— current liabilities and long-term liabilities.

Current liabilities are a company's short-term financial obligations that are due within one year. For Bob, these include:

I)   Accounts Payable: this is the money Bob needs to pay to some of his vendors.

II) Accrued Expenses: these are some of the expenses like electricity bills and gas bills that are owed by Bob's donut shop.

III) Unearned Revenue: this is the revenue for which Bob has received money but has not delivered the donuts yet.

Long-term liabilities are a company's financial obligations that are due after one year. These generally include things like bank loans and notes payable. The total of current liabilities and long-term liabilities is called total liabilities.

As we saw from the accounting equation, liabilities are followed by equity. This is depicted in the balance sheet as well.

The equity component of the balance sheet includes:

I) Retained Earnings: these are the leftover earnings of a company after paying all dividends to share- holders.
II) Common Stock: this is the amount of capital that Bob has personally invested in the company.

The two sides of the balance sheet—assets and liabilities/equity—will always match in the end, as depicted by the accounting equation that we looked at before.

CASH FLOW STATEMENT

Bob told me that his cash flow statement gave him an idea about how changes in the balance sheet accounts affected his cash account during the period. It basically is a reconciliation of the beginning cash balances and ending cash balances. It shows the investors and creditors what transactions affected the cash accounts and how effectively and efficiently a company can use its cash to finance its operations and expansions. Investors also determine from this statement whether the company is liquid enough to pay its bills as they come due. In other words, does the company have a good cash flow?

Bob Vance Donuts Inc. Statement of Cash Flows for the Quarter ended December 31, 1975	$	$
Cash Flows from Operating Activities		
Net Income		129,500
Adjustments to reconcile net income to net cash provided by operating activities:		
Depreciation on Fixed Assets		20,000
(Increase) decrease in current assets:		
Accounts receivable		(3,000)
Inventory		(398,000)
Prepaid Expenses		(10,000)
(Increase) decrease in current liabilities:		
Accounts Payable		490,000
Accrued Expenses and Unearned Revenues		14,500
Net Cash Provided by Operating Activities		243,000
Cash Flows from Investing Activities		
Purchase of Property and Equipment		(101,000)
Net Cash used in Investing Activities		(101,000)
Cash Flows from Financing Activities		
Proceeds from line of credit		0
Payments on line of credit		100,000
Proceeds from long-term debt		995,000
Payments on long-term debt		0
Net Cash Provided(Used) in Financing Activities		1,095,000
Net Increase/(Decrease) in Cash		328,000
Beginning Cash Balance		0
Ending Cash Balance		**328,000**

The cash flow statement is divided into three main sections: cash flows from operating activities, investing activities, and financing activities.

1. Adding back noncash charges such as deprecia- tion that were subtracted before. These noncash charges have to be added back to reflect the "true" cash generated by the operating activities.

2. Adding/subtracting changes in working capital accounts, like current assets and liabilities. Increase in current assets like inventory means that the company has paid cash for it,

so this is subtracted, as it is a cash outflow. Following this logic, a decrease in current assets is an inflow. However, a decrease in current liabilities like accounts payable means the company paid the debt, and so cash outflow would be triggered. Similarly, increase in liabilities will be considered a cash inflow.

Investing Activities:

Cash flows from investing activities consist of cash inflows/ outflows from sales and purchases of long-term assets. In other words, you can think of this section as the company investing in itself. For Bob, this included investment in his property and equipment.

Financing Activities:

Cash flows from financing consist of cash transactions that affect the long-term liabilities and equity accounts.

Transactions like proceeds from short-term or long- term debt are cash inflows and will increase the cash balances. Transactions like payment of debt will mean there is cash outflow and will reduce the cash balances In other words, the financing section on the statement represents the amount of cash collected from issuing stock or taking out loans and the amount of cash disbursed to pay dividends and long-term debt. You can think of financing activities as ways a company finances its operations, either through long-term debt or equity financing.

Financing cash flows are calculated by adding up the changes in all the long-term liability and equity accounts.

Here is a simple tip Bob used to remember which transactions go into which section:

Operating Activities: Includes all activities that are reported on the income statement under operating income or expenses.

Investing Activities: Includes all cash transactions used to buy or sell long-term assets. Think of these as the company investing in itself.

Financing Activities: Includes all cash transactions that affect long-term liabilities and equity. Whenever long-term debt or equity is involved, it is considered a financing activity.

RATIO ANALYSIS AND INTERPRETING THE FINANCIAL STATEMENTS

Understanding how the financial statements are constructed is usually the first step when investing in a particular company. The next step is to analyze key investment metrics and financial ratios to make sense of those financial statements.

Some of the important ratios that a value investor usually looks at when deciding whether to invest in a particular company are:

1. Price-to-Cash-Flow Ratio

Some people prefer to use this ratio instead of the price- to-earnings ratio since it provides a better picture of the company's cash flow operations per share.

2. Price-to-Earnings Ratio

This ratio is likely the most famous ratio in the world. It's a quick-and-easy way to see how cheap or costly a stock is compared to its peers.

The P/E is the amount of money the market is willing to pay for every dollar in earnings a company generates. You have to decide whether that amount is too high, a bargain, or somewhere in between.

3. PEG Ratio

Sometimes the P/E ratio of a company might be lower compared to its peers. This doesn't necessarily mean it is a better investment, since it could very well be the case that the growth opportunities of the peer companies are higher. This is why we take the P/E ratio one step further and use the price/earnings-to-growth ratio instead. This is simply the P/E ratio divided by the growth.

4. Asset Turnover Ratio

This ratio gauges the revenue generated by each dollar of assets a company owns. It's a good way of judging how well it has been using its assets compared to its peers.

5. Current Ratio

This serves as a test of financial strength. It can give you an idea as to whether a company has too much or too little cash on hand to meet its obligations. It's figured by dividing current assets by current liabilities.

6. Quick Ratio

The quick ratio is a more stringent way to assess the financial strength of a company and its ability to meet obligations. It subtracts inventory from current assets before dividing by current liabilities. The point is that a company may need a good deal of time to liquidate its assets before the money can be used to cover what it owes.

7. Debt-to-Equity Ratio

The debt-to-equity ratio lets you compare the total stockholders' equity of a company (the amount they have invested in the company plus retained earnings) to its total liabilities. Stockholders' equity is sometimes viewed as the net worth of a company from the viewpoint of its owners.

This ratio basically tells you how highly leveraged the company is. The higher the leverage is, the higher the risk is since the company would have a higher interest burden to pay.

8. Gross Profit Margin

The gross profit margin lets you know how much of a company's profit is available as a percentage of revenue to meet its expenses. Subtract the cost of goods sold from total sales. Divide the result by total sales.

9. Net Profit Margin

This tells you how much a company makes for every dollar of its revenue. For instance, an 8% profit margin means that the company's leftover earnings after it has paid all its expenses is 8 cents for every dollar of goods/ services sold.

10. Interest Coverage Ratio

This ratio is important for analyzing companies that carry a lot of debt. It lets you know how much money is there to cover the interest expense a company incurs on the money it owes every year.

11. Return on Assets

This ratio tells you how much profit a company generated for each dollar it has in assets. It is calculated by dividing net profits by total assets. It measures how well the company is using its assets to generate a profit. This ratio is therefore useful when comparing performance with peers.

12. Return on Equity

This is probably among the most important ratios that investors are concerned about. It reveals how much profit a company earned compared to the total amount of stockholders' equity found on its balance sheet.

There are many other standard investment ratios/ metrics that an investor can look into. Some financially savvy value investors like Warren Buffett also have their own customized ratios, which have been working well for them over the past many years.

Whichever combination of ratios you will be using to determine whether the company is financially strong enough to be invested in, one thing is important—do your own research!

A value investor does not invest on mere hearsay from others. They do their own research and picks her own winner stocks!

USING NUMBERS FOR INVESTING

I￼T'S GOOD THAT YOU NOW know a bit about financial statements. This will help you greatly in making astute investment decisions. You will be able to distinguish the good-performing companies from the underperforming ones. You can now also make the distinction between growth companies and value companies.

Growth stocks are better for making capital gains over the long run, since these companies are involved in a competitive, growing business environment. Most of the technology-related companies, like Amazon, Apple, and Tesla, can be characterized as growth companies. These companies are more prone to economic cycles like a recession, with their earnings taking a severe hit. They rarely are known for paying consistent dividends. They are also usually trading at a higher P/E, PEG, and P/B multiple. Meanwhile, value stocks are companies that are involved in a relatively stable and predictable business, such as Procter & Gamble or Johnson & Johnson. Their balance sheets are somewhat resistant to economic cycles and are also known to provide consistent dividends for their investors. These stocks are usually trading at a lower P/E, PEG, and P/B multiple compared to growth stocks.

Whichever company you invest in, be sure to have a well-diversified portfolio. My dad had his fair share of wins and losses in the equity market, but because his stock portfolio had over thirty stocks in it, he was well diversified and never really got too affected by a few stocks performing negatively.

Within his portfolio, he wanted to keep stocks that had little-to-no correlation with each other in terms of the businesses and industries they were operating in. He was never a fan of betting on any one specific industry and giving it an unfairly high allocation in his overall portfolio. One thing was sure though—he never bought a stock without having done concrete research on it. He would look at not only how the stock would perform individually but how it would complement his entire portfolio as well. He would call this concept "beta" and would later explain to us how regression models were used to calculate this.

Before we get into regression, you need to know what a cause-and-effect relationship is.

CAUSE-AND-EFFECT RELATIONSHIP

To explain this concept, my dad took me and my brother to our backyard and showed us two contrasting areas of land where he used to grow strawberries. He explained that both these areas were taken care of in the same way except for one difference. In one of the areas, he used to put in fertilizer, and in the other area, he didn't.

In the area where the fertilizer was used, there were a lot more strawberries than the area where fertilizer was not being used. He explained this in terms of a cause- and-effect relationship. The fertilizer was the cause, or the independent variable, and the higher output of strawberries was the effect, or the dependent variable, in this scenario.

REGRESSION

Regression is simply an expression of the mathematical function of the cause-and-effect relationship described above.

The effect, also known as the dependent variable, is represented by a y variable, whereas the cause, being an independent variable, is represented by an x variable.

There are two basic types of regressions. The first is a simple linear regression, and the second is multiple linear regression. Simple linear regression models employ one independent variable to understand or predict the result of the dependent variable (y). In my dad's example, fertilizer usage is the single independent variable, and the output of strawberries is the dependent variable.

Multiple linear regression considers two or more independent variables to understand or predict the result of the dependent variable. A second variable could be anything else my dad can alter in his strawberry-gardening experiment. For instance, the amount of water given to the two areas of land can be considered a second independent variable. We can then include the use of water along with the use of fertilizer as the two independent variables to understand the dependent variable, which is the output of strawberries in this case.

CAPITAL ASSET PRICING MODEL (CAPM)

The most widely used application of this regression concept is in the capital asset pricing model (CAPM), which is used to calculate the expected return from assets, especially stocks.

My dad showed us the below equation, which baffled us at first impression, but he walked us through it in very simple words, which I am going to try to repeat here with you as well.

The mathematical expression for CAPM is as follows:

ERi = Rf + üL (5P ï 5I

where:

ERi = expected return of investment Rf = risk-free rate

üi = beta of the investment

(&3N¦3G) = NBSLFU SJTL QSFNJVN

The first concept that he talked about was that every investor wants to be compensated for the time value of money and the risk that they have taken by investing. We interrupted him immediately and asked him what the time value of money is.

Our dad always believed in creating curiosity inside us to teach us new things in life. To teach us what the time value of money is, he asked us another interesting question. Does $10 have more value today or one year from now? This got us confused, and we said that $10 today would have the same value as $10 one year later.

He shook his head in disagreement and told us that $10 today has a higher value than $10 one year later because today's money has a potential earning capacity. This means that today's money can be used to create more money. Time value of money (TVM) is one of the fundamental concepts of finance.

He brought the discussion back to CAPM and continued by saying that the risk-free rate in the CAPM formula factors in for this time value of money component. Meanwhile, the other variables in the formula account for the impact of higher risk that the investor is taking on from a particular stock.

5IF CFUB (€J) MFUT VT LOPX UIF SJTLJOFTT MFWFM PG BO

investment against the market. The beta itself is a number that is calculated through a regression model, but for simplicity's sake, we won't go into any depth on how it is calculated.

All you need to know is that if an investment in a particular stock is considered riskier than the market, then its beta would be greater than one.

This would mean that if the beta of a stock is 1.2, then its value would rise or fall by 12% if the overall market observes an increase or decrease of 10%. On the other hand, if an investment is less risky than the market, its beta would be less than 1. For instance, a beta of 0.8 would mean that the market would observe an increase or decrease of 10%, while the stock would experience a rise or fall of only 8% in comparison.

The beta of the particular stock you are investing in is then multiplied by the market risk premium. What is market risk premium? &3N ¦ 3G JT DPOTJEFSFE UIF EJGGFSFODF JO SFUVSO anticipated from the market and the risk-free rate. So, if someone wants to invest in an equity market, he will most likely want to get a higher return on his investment as compared to someone who invests in only T-bills earning a risk-free rate. This is because the market investor wants to get rewarded for the additional risk that he is taking on. Therefore, ERm, or market return, will be always higher than the risk-free rate, or Rf.

Finally, the risk-free rate is added to the product obtained as a result of multiplying the beta with the market risk premium. The final result is the expected return that can be used to find the true value of an asset.

The purpose of CAPM is to gauge whether the valuation of a stock is fair when the time value of money and its risk is compared against its expected return. Let's go through a simplified example to understand this process.

For instance, if you want to buy 1 share of Coca-Cola stock with $10 today, then you can use CAPM to decide whether it would be wise to buy the stock. As Coca-Cola is a relatively stable company, which means its price fluctuations are much less volatile than the market, let us assume that it has a beta of 0.6. Also assume that the risk-free rate is 4%, and you expect the market to rise by 10%. The expected return for Coca-Cola would be 7.6% based on the CAPM formula below.

$$7\ 6\% = 4\% + 0\ 6\ \ddot{}\ (10\%\ \vdots\ 4\%)$$

We are only halfway through the process of determining whether we should invest in Coca-Cola. Let's assume that we will be holding the stock for five years and that at the end of five years, the stock price of Coca- Cola would be $16.

We would use the expected return obtained from the CAPM formula to discount the stock price of Coca-Cola after five years and determine whether we should buy the stock or not.

Discounting is the opposite of compounding, which was discussed at length in Chapter One. Discounting is the method used to determine the present value of a cash flow that is expected in the future. We have already discussed that $10 today has a higher value than $10 tomorrow or a year later due to the concept of the time value of money.

In our case, we would use the following formula to discount the stock price of Coca-Cola after five years:

$$\mathbf{NPV} = \frac{R_t}{(1 + i)^t}$$

where:

NPV = net present value
Rt = net cash flow at time t ($16) i = discount rate (7.6%)
t = time of the cash flow (5 years)

If we apply this formula, then the NPV would come would come out to be $11.09. This means that the stock price of $16 after 5 years is equivalent to $11.09 today, and at the price of $10, the stock price of Coca-Cola is undervalued and should be bought.

LAW OF AVERAGES

Bernard Baruch, a renowned financier of the nineteenth century, said, "Only liars manage to always be out during bad times and in during good times." This quote is a clear reflection that it is next to impossible to time the market successfully to earn healthy and consistent returns.

An intelligent person may like to think that they have the foresight to sell their investment before a market crash and buy it back when the market has bottomed out. However, markets are very dynamic, and it is very challenging to predict their highs and lows. There can be circumstances where you can miss the rebound phase of the market and buy your position at a price that can be higher than the price at which you sold. This would be termed as selling low and buying high and stands against the basics of investing.

DOLLAR-COST AVERAGING

Fortunately, the uncertainty of the market can be hedged by investing at regular intervals over a long period. This technique is known as the "dollar-cost averaging" and is regarded as a proven measure against volatility in the market.

This technique derives from the law of averages. The law of averages states that in the long run, random events will even out and balance any deviations of the past and bring them close to the average. Under this assumption, investors invest at regular periods to minimize volatility in their investments.

By investing over a long period at regular intervals, you will be able to benefit by buying shares when markets are down. In the end, the average price per share can be expected to be lower as opposed to investing all the money at the same time. Furthermore, the dollar-cost averaging technique stops the investor from timing the market and thus results in lower speculative play.

Let's go through an example to understand this concept more clearly. To demonstrate this concept, my father gave me two choices. The first option was that he could give me a lump sum of $6,000 anytime in one go in the next six months, and I could use that money to buy the stock of Coca-Cola. The second option was that he could give me $1,000 every month for six months to buy Coke stock.

The table below shows that the dollar-cost averaging technique resulted in a better average as opposed to making the complete purchase at the same time.

If I had opted to buy all $6,000 worth of Coke stock in one go in any of the four highlighted months (February, March, April, and May), I would have purchased at a higher price than the $105.89 obtained as a result of dollar-cost averaging technique.

Month	Investment	Per Share Price	No. of Shares Bought
January	$1,000	$101	9.90
February	$1,000	$107	9.35
March	$1,000	$108	9.26
April	$1,000	$110	9.09
May	$1,000	$108	9.26
June	$1,000	$102	9.80
Total	$6,000	$105.89	56.66

A 401(k) plan is a perfect example of a dollar-cost averaging technique. An employee can decide beforehand that a certain amount from their salary is diverted toward an index or mutual fund.

It must be noted that the dollar-cost averaging technique works in your favor only when the price of the underlying investment is expected to rise over the longer period. It is not a hedge against consistent declining prices. Therefore, it is very crucial to understand the fundamentals of a particular stock before carrying out the dollar-cost averaging technique. You don't want to be in a scenario where you get stuck buying more of a "failing" company's stock instead of actually liquidating or exiting the stock.

CHAPTER 5

MAKING SENSE OF CHARTS AND TRADING PATTERNS

So FAR, WE HAVE MOSTLY talked about the fundamental school of thought in investing. But did you know that this is just one side of the coin? Fundamental investors are the long-term investors who have garnered a good reputation for themselves by consistently achieving a decent return from the market by investing based on fundamentals like revenue, earnings, valuations, and industry dynamics.

There is another type of investor who belongs to the technical-analysis school of thought. He is an avid believer that price movements can be calculated by historical data, primarily through price and volume. He employs the top-down approach, where he identifies securities that are expected to perform strongly based on their technical analysis.

Before we dive deep in the world of technical analysis, let us cover some basic need-to-know concepts first.

MONEYLINE VS. POINT SPREAD BETTING

The simplest bet to place in a sport is predicting the winner in a game between two teams or two opponents. This is known as moneyline betting. The bet is based on no handicap involved. For a better understanding, let's go through a simple example.

In the National Football League (NFL) 2021 season, the Jacksonville Jaguars have scheduled to take on Arizona Cardinals on September 26, 2021, at TIAA Bank Field, home to the Jacksonville Jaguars. The Arizona Cardinals have won the first two games of the season and are looking for the best start to the NFL season since 2015. On the other hand, Jacksonville has lost the first two contests of this season.

From this brief analysis, it would seem that the Cardinals are the favorite to win the contest. When a winner is outright obvious in a contest, then the odds are not favorable. Such is the case in this scenario as well. According to bookmakers, the odds of Cardinals winning are 380. On the other hand, the odds of Jaguars winning are at +290.

To win $100 by betting on the Cardinals, you would have to put in $380. It's a negative moneyline and usually associated with the favorite in a contest. To calculate the reward, we should divide the odds by 100 and then divide it by the amount we are betting. For instance, if we put up $20 on the Cardinals winning, then we would get a reward of ($20 / 3.8) = $5.26 on top of the $20 bet.

Conversely, the Jaguars have a positive moneyline, and usually, these odds are associated with an underdog in a contest. To obtain the reward of placing a bet of $20, just divide the odds by 100, and then multiply it by the amount that is put on the bet. In our case, a $20 bet would result in a reward of ($20 x 2.9) = $58 on top of the $20 bet. Although these odds may look very enticing, the bet seems illogical given the big difference in the qualities of the two teams.

The fun goes out of the moneyline wager when a team is anticipated to be an outright winner. To get things interesting, point spread betting comes into play. The point spread bet assumes a team will win by more than a certain number of points to make good on that bet. On the other hand, a losing team is expected to lose by less than a certain number of points to win that bet. Let's go through an example to better understand this.

One of the point spread bets offered by bookmakers on the Cardinals versus Jaguars game is 7.5 (115) for the Cardinals and +7.5 (107) for the Jaguars. This means that the Cardinals are the 7.5-point favorite. Those betting on the Cardinals (7.5) would need the Bird Gang to win by 8 points or more; otherwise, they would lose their bet. However, if the Cardinals win by 8 points or more, then every bet of $115 will get a reward of $100. As for the Jaguars (+7.5), they are the underdogs, and if they win the game or even lose the game against the Cardinals by fewer than 7.5 points, then every bet of $107 will get a reward of $100.

IMPLIED PROBABILITY AND VIG

Through moneyline betting, we can better understand the concept of implied probability, which tells us whether we should place a bet. Let's carry on with the above example of the Jaguars and Cardinals. The Cardinals' odds stand at 380, which we already know means that to win $100, $380 needs to be put up. Implied probability is calculated by dividing the risk with reward. In our case, the $380 stake is the risk, and the reward is the $380 coming back along with the $100 win, which equals $480. Thus, the implied probability of the Cardinals winning is ($380 / $480) = 79.17%. In reality, if you believe that the Cardinals have a higher chance of winning, then there is an opportunity for you to place your bet.

Meanwhile, the odds of the Jaguars winning are at +290. This means that the risk would be the $100 stake put up to place the bet, and the reward would be the $100 stake coming back along with the $290 winnings. Thus, the implied probability of the Jaguars winning is ($100 / $390) = 25.64%. If you think that the Jaguars have a higher likelihood of winning the game, only then should you place the bet.

Did you notice that when you add the two implied probabilities, the result comes out to be 104.81%? The reason it is higher than 100% is that it involves the bookmaker's profit, which is commonly known as the vig. To remove the impact of the vig from the odds, divide 79.17% / 104.81% = 75.54% and 25.64% / 104.81% = 24.46%. Now if you add both the implied probabilities, the result would come out to be 100%, assuming that the vig is distributed equally between both odds. When you convert the implied probabilities, the odds come out to be 309 for the Cardinals and +309 for the Jaguars. Our calculation revealed that the bookmaker kept a 4.81% profit.

EXPECTED VALUE

The expected value is the average profit that the bookmaker is making from our staked amount. We know that the Cardinals' odds stand at 380, it would pay ($100/ 3.8) = $26.31, and our chance of winning is 75.54%. Meanwhile, the probability of losing is 24.46%, and we would lose the $100 staked. When all these numbers are put in the formula as (.7554 x $26.31) – (.2446 x $100) = -$4.58, this means we have an expected return on investment (ROI) of 4.58%. In other words, the bookmaker would make a profit of 4.58% on every $100 staked.

Let's reverse the tables and calculate the expected value for the Jaguars. We know the Jaguars' odds were +290, a $100 stake would pay a reward of $290, and the chance of winning for the Jaguars is 24.46%. When we insert all the values in the formula as (.2446 x 290) – (.7554 x 100) = $4.61, this means that we have an expected ROI of 4.61%. In other words, the bookmaker would make a profit of 4.61% on every $100 staked.

CANDLESTICK CHARTS

Decoding the candlestick charts was something that my dad taught me. He used to say that key information about the short-term price movement of a stock can be obtained from the candlestick charts.

The candlestick charts show the opening, closing, high, and low prices for the day. The wide part is also known as the real body, and it shows the difference between opening and closing prices for a particular day. When the real body is black or filled with a color like red, this means that the opening price was higher than the closing price for the day. This type of candle is known as the down candle, as the stock closed the day in the red. If the real body is empty or filled with a positive color like green, then this means that the opening price was lower than the closing price. This is an example of an up candle. Both these types of candles are shown in the figure below.

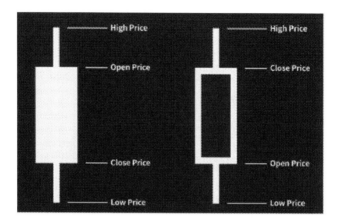

The real body is connected to the high and low prices for the day by the shadows or wicks. If there is a down candle and the upper shadow is close to the real body, then this would mean that the highest price for the day was near the opening price for that day. On the other hand, a short shadow on an up candle would show that the highest price for the day was near the closing price for that respective day. Shadows can be long or short.

Up-and-down price fluctuations create candlesticks. To a layman, these price fluctuations may look random, but on numerous occasions, these price movements create a pattern that traders employ for trading purposes. These patterns can be either bearish or bullish. A bearish pattern anticipates that a decline in stock price is likely to take place. Meanwhile, a bullish pattern foresees a rise in stock price. The pattern doesn't have to be followed 100% of the time, as the pattern is based on historical price movement and the stock doesn't need to follow the price movement as predicted by the pattern. Let's go through some candlestick patterns that are employed for analysis and trading purposes.

BEARISH ENGULFING CANDLE

This pattern comes on the candlestick charts when the sellers start to dominate the market during an uptrend. This pattern anticipates lower prices going forward. In this pattern, a small up candle can be followed by a dominant down candle that sweeps overs or "engulfs" the smaller up candle. The pattern can be critical because it shows that the power in the market has shifted from the buyers to the sellers and the prices can continue to fall. This pattern is shown in the chart below.

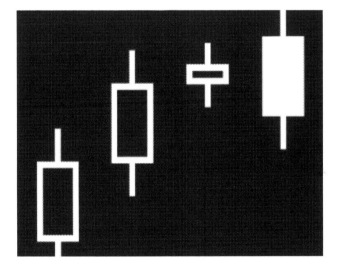

A strong bearish engulfing pattern comes into play when the real body of the down candle completely overshadows the previous small up candle. However, if the stock is trading within a range in a choppy market, then the importance of the bearish engulfing pattern is much less.

BULLISH ENGULFING CANDLE

When the buyers get back the power from the sellers during a bearish period, the bullish engulfing pattern is seen on the candlestick chart. This pattern anticipates the price will rise and bounce back from the slump. In this pattern, a small down candle is followed by a big up candle that overshadows the smaller down candle, as shown in the chart below.

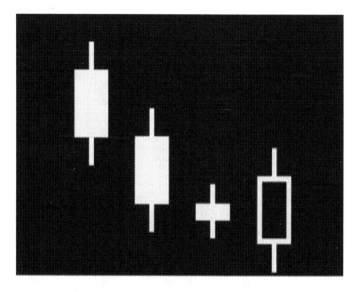

For a strong bullish engulfing candle, it is necessary that the real body of the up candle completely overshadow the previous small down candle.

There are hundreds of other candlestick patterns that can be learned and examined.

MOVING AVERAGE

Moving average (MA) is one of the first tools that our father introduced to us when looking at the stock price charts for the very first time. Moving average is widely popular because it removes the noise created by short-term stock price fluctuations and provides price data based on continuously updated average prices. The moving average can be over a period as required by the trader, like 10 minutes, 10 days, or 10 weeks, depending on the short-term or long-term trading strategy. Traders also have the option to use different types of moving averages.

At first glimpse, the moving average line on a stock price chart can reveal the overall direction the stock price is heading. If the moving average is heading upward, then this would mean that the stock price is rising. If it is moving down, then this would mean that the stock price is falling. If the moving average is moving sideways, then this means the stock is trading within a range.

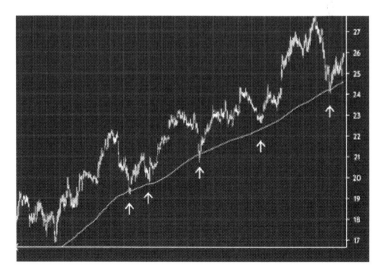

Moving averages are known to act as support or resistance. When the stock price is on the rise, then a 50-day, 100-day, or 200-day moving average can act as a floor from where the prices recover. This is shown in the chart below. Meanwhile, when there is a trend of the stock price moving down, the moving average may act as a ceiling, and the stock price would decline after hitting the moving average price. It is not necessary that the price of the stock would immediately rise or fall after hitting the moving average. The price may slightly cross the moving average before reversing its trend.

Moving averages can be computed in various manners. The simple moving average (SMA) just adds the most recent values and divides them by the frequency. For instance, in the case of the 10-day simple moving average, the closing price of the most recent 10 days is added and then divided by 10 to obtain the 10-day simple moving average.

Another renowned moving average is the exponential moving average (EMA). Its computation is more complica- ted and gives more weight to recent prices during the computation of the moving average. This makes EMA more reactive to recent price changes as opposed to SMA, as shown in the chart below.

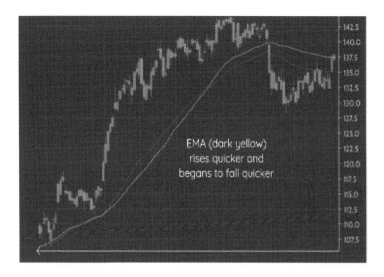

EMA (dark yellow)
rises quicker and
begans to fall quicker

Trading software provides all types of moving averages for all durations at a click of a button, and thus it is not necessary to know exactly how various moving averages are calculated.

No one type of moving average is better than the other. In some cases, EMA may help more in predicting the stock price movements, and in some cases, SMA may provide a better outlook.

Traders employ 10, 20, 50, 100, and 200 as common moving average lengths. The length of time can be minutes, days, or weeks depending on the time frame of the trader. For instance, for a short-term trade, a 10-day moving average would be more suitable compared to a 100-day moving average, because it would have less lag when prices fluctuate. The time required to signal a potential reversal is known as the lag. Thus, a ten-day moving average would give more reversal signs compared to a 10-day moving average, as shown in the chart below.

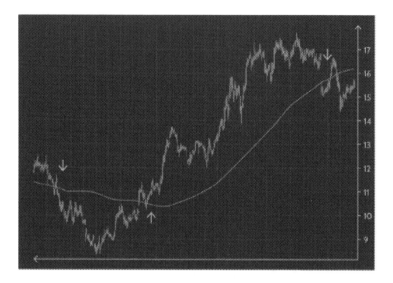

Another popular strategy used by the trader is applying two moving averages to a stock price chart. One is a short-term moving average, like the 10-day moving average, and one is long term, like the 100-day moving average. A buy signal is shown on the stock price chart when the short-term moving average crosses above the long-term moving average. Among the trading circles, this is known as the "golden cross."

On the other hand, if the short-term moving average crosses below the long-term moving average, then it considered a selling signal, and this indicates that the stock price is on a downward trend. This is an instance of "dead" or "death cross." The example of the golden cross and death cross is shown in the chart below.

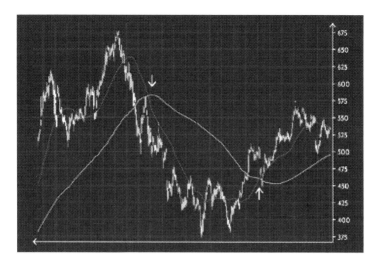

After this brief discussion on moving averages, it must be pointed out that the calculation is based on historical data and does not have any predictive element to it. That is why in some cases, the moving averages can be just random.

This means that market may respond to moving average as support or resistance, but there can be instances where moving average gets thrown out the window. This random nature comes into play heavily when the stock is trading within a range with no visible trend and the price is continuously rising and falling. This creates multiple trend reversals and crossovers as well. At a time like this, it is best to step away from moving average techniques and employ other trading techniques.

BOLLINGER BANDS

The Bollinger Band builds upon the concept of moving averages. Under this technique, two trend lines are plotted around the SMA. The trend lines highlight the positive and negative two-standard deviations. Usually, the 20-day SMA is employed, where the closing price of the past 20 consecutive days is added and then divided by 20 for every data point on the chart. After that, the standard deviation for every data point is obtained. Standard deviation is the measure of volatility and computed by taking the square root of the variance and shows how spread out numbers are from the mean. The standard deviation is multiplied by two and then added and subtracted to the SMA to obtain the upper and lower bands.

When the market is more volatile, the gap between the SMA and the upper and lower bands increases. Meanwhile, during periods of stability, the upper and lower bands come closer to the SMA.

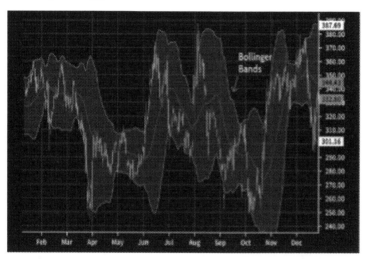

One of the most common beliefs related to the Bollinger Band is that when the stock is close to the upper band, it means that the stock is overbought. Meanwhile, when the stock price is close to the lower band, then it means that the stock is oversold.

The squeeze is another common concept related to the Bollinger Band. This is observed when the upper and lower bands come close to the SMA. This signifies a period of stability and is considered by traders as a precursor to a period of higher volatility going forward. On the other hand, if the bands move farther apart, there is a higher likelihood that the volatility will decrease in the future.

Nearly 90% of the price actions take place between the two bands. Whenever there is a breakout from the higher or lower Bollinger Band, it is considered a significant event. However, it must be highlighted that when the price crosses the higher or lower band, it does not reflect a buy or sell signal. Furthermore, Bollinger Bands are not themselves a trading system. They need to be associated with various other types of data.

MOVING AVERAGE CONVERGENCE DIVERGENCE (MACD)

The moving average convergence divergence (MACD) is an oscillating technical indicator. An oscillating indicator changes over some time and stays inside a band. In the case of MACD, it hovers above and below zero. The MACD is shown on the histogram below the stock price chart.

If the MACD lines are above zero for a significant amount of time, then the stock price can be anticipated to move upward. This means that when the MACD is above zero, then it's a buy signal. However, if the MACD lines remain below zero for a significant amount of time, then the stock price can be anticipated to move downward. This means that when the MACD is below zero, then it's a sell signal.

More buy-and-sell signals can be obtained from signal-line crossovers. An MACD chart has two lines—a fast line and a slow line. When the fast line crosses and moves above the slow line, then it is considered a buy signal. Meanwhile, when the fast line crosses and moves below the slow line, then it is considered a sell signal.

RELATIVE STRENGTH INDEX (RSI)

Another popular oscillating indicator is the relative strength index (RSI). It moves between 0 and 100. The two main interpretations of RSI are that when it is above 70, it means that the stock has been overbought, and the stock price is likely to fall, and on the other hand, if the RSI falls below 30, then the stock is oversold, and its stock price is likely to rise.

When the stock is experiencing an uptrend, then the RSI can be expected to remain above 70 for a significant time. Meanwhile, during downtrends, the RSI can be anticipated to remain below 30 for a lengthy amount of time.

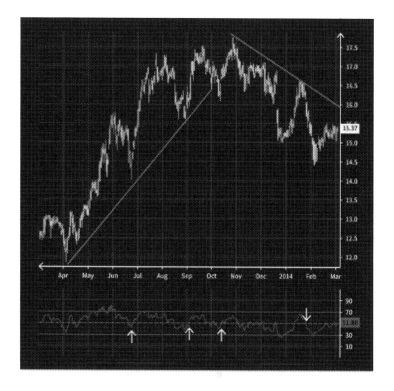

ON-BALANCE VOLUME (OBV)

The on-balance volume (OBV) indicator shows information about the volume in a single line. It is calculated by adding the volume on days when the stock was up and subtracting the volume on days when the stock price was down. The OBV confirms a particular trend. For instance, if the stock price is rising, then the same should happen with the OBV as well. Meanwhile, a falling stock price would be accompanied by a declining OBV.

There are some instances when the OBV is rising but the stock price is not. In such circumstances, the price will soon follow OBV and start to rise. Meanwhile, if the OBV has reached its peak or starts to fall at the time when the stock price is rising, then this would indicate that the stock price has also peaked and can be heading toward a decline or pullback. Meanwhile, if the stock price is plummeting and its OBV is rising or flatlined, then the stock price can be expected to be bottomed out and on its way to recovery.

A COMBINATION OF FUNDAMENTAL AND TECHNICAL ANALYSIS

Technical analysis differs significantly from fundamental analysis as it takes stock price and volume as the two main inputs to make its prediction. It is assumed that all the fundamentals are already incorporated in the stock price and thus do not require a look. Traders are not looking to calculate the intrinsic value of a stock but instead looking for trends and patterns that can give them a peek at how the stock price will perform in the future.

An intelligent investor combines the strength of both these strategies to better comprehend the market and anticipate the price movements correctly. For instance, volume trends can be brought into play to understand whether investors are accumulating or offloading a particular stock when there is a spike in volumes. A spike in volume can also highlight the market's interest in a stock. A high-volume stock on the rise has more eyeballs in the market. If the volume starts to fall, then it means that the stock is losing interest and a reversal can be on the way Although fundamental investing is done with an intention of a long-term holding period, suitable entry and exit positions can be found by employing technical- analysis parameters. Furthermore, technical-analysis tools can also provide an insight into how the stock reacts to various types of news like the release of its earnings or some other periodic economic data.

a debt trap and then spend the rest of their working lives paying it off bit by bit.

That is one way of living your life!

The other way is to implement the principles of wealth creation that I will teach you in this closing chapter. In the previous chapters of this book, I focused more on the different research tools, business concepts, and aspects of investments. Now I will show you how to use all that knowledge that you have developed so far to create generational wealth for yourself and your family.

Let me first introduce this all-important matrix, which I believe is essential for every kid to know early on in his or her life. You won't ever find this in any financial textbook you will read in college later on.

So pay close attention!

CHAPTER 6

UNDERSTANDING THE PHILOSOPHY OF WEALTH CREATION

THE IMPORTANT QUESTION THAT YOU need to ask yourself at this stage is whether you really want to build generational wealth in your life—the kind of wealth that passes on to the next generation so that they don't get stuck in the rat race. Forming generational wealth needs only one person to financially educate him or herself about wealth creation, and then the later generations will reap the rewards.

I emphasized in the opening chapter of this book that many people get stuck in the rat race of "selling" their working hours to make a living. Now don't get me wrong— that is a perfectly good way to start creating money, and you can then embark on your journey to wealth creation as your income grows. However, for most people, the journey of wealth creation ends as soon as they start upgrading their lifestyles to match their incomes. They start to buy bigger houses, bigger cars, and expensive vacations they clearly cannot afford yet. They get stuck in a debt trap and then spend the rest of their working lives paying it off bit by bit.

That is one way of living your life!

The other way is to implement the principles of wealth creation that I will teach you in this closing chapter. In the previous chapters of this book, I focused more on the different research tools, business concepts, and aspects of investments. Now I will show you how to use all that knowledge that you have developed so far to create generational wealth for yourself and your family.

Let me first introduce this all-important matrix, which I believe is essential for every kid to know early on in his or her life. You won't ever find this in any financial textbook you will read in college later on.

So pay close attention!

Kitchen Income	Investor
Asset Creation	Institution

The four quadrants above (kitchen income, asset creation, investor, and institution) represent the different financial phases of your life that you can possibly go through when you grow up. It is important to understand which phase you are currently in and what you need to do to get to the next phase.

The first stage of life is what I describe as making enough money so that you are able to afford basic rent, household supplies, food, and health care for your family. I call this your kitchen income or the money you need for basic sustenance. For some people, this is the first and often the last financial stage of life they get to witness. This might be due to a variety of reasons, such as not being able to secure a high-paying job due to lack of skills and formal education. This person is never able to save enough money and mostly lives paycheck to paycheck.

Others quickly move into their second financial stage in life, i.e., asset creation. Many people eventually successfully pay off their mortgages and now have a house to their name, which will typically be worth $200,000 or more. They will be close to their retirement age and will be for the first time debt free after many years. All their hard work and struggles throughout life have amounted to them now having a debt-free home in which they can spend the remainder of their living years after retirement. The government will give them a steady pension, and they can retire in peace, spending the rest of their lives with their loved ones close by.

Many people don't know much about the third financial phase of life because it requires you to be financially savvy, and people just don't make the effort to educate themselves, as it takes time and experience. I have many friends who are in marketing and sales careers, and when I discuss personal finance and investments with them, they tell me that they don't know much about it because it is not their field. Well, sorry to burst your bubble, but everyone must know about personal finance and investments. It is the stage of your life where you make your money work for you and create more money. And you finally stop "selling" your working hours.

This stage is called the investor stage, and it is a tricky one, I will admit. Some people will jump into this phase without having the required knowledge about how investments work. Guess what? They lose their entire life savings because of "speculative bets" without proper research, guidance, advice, and knowledge. People who don't know how to manage their investment portfolios, diversify risk, and do the required due diligence will jump into an investment on hearsay or in fear of missing out. This type of investment strategy never works out, and that is why they lose all of their investment.

A similar event occurred back in 2007–2008, when many families lost their investments due to panic selling, risky investments, and undiversified portfolios. These people become "anti-investing," and because of their personal bad experiences, they also started to discourage others from investing.

You need to shut out this noise from your life!

In the previous chapters, I have gone over all the basic investment fundamentals you will need to make sound investment decisions and manage your risk. As long as you implement everything taught to you in this book, you will do pretty well with investing overall. Hold diversified portfolios and have a long-term perspective, and investing becomes easy. Even a monkey can do it! The investor stage, unlike the previous two stages of kitchen income and asset creation, is not age dependent. If you started investing at a very young age—let us say when you were eleven years old, like Warren Buffett did— you will reap the rewards earlier than others. Being in the investors group also has a lot of tax advantages that we won't go into much detail about in this book, but all you need to know is that you will enjoy fewer taxes imposed on you by the government. This will help you compound your money even faster compared to a blue- or white-collar salaried individual whose paycheck is taxed at source.

With all the different investment concepts and techniques taught to you in the previous chapters, you will now be able to make wiser and more financially savvy decisions to master this third financial stage of life. This book is only meant to serve as a fire starter in your journey of seeking financial wisdom. By no means is it meant to be the only book you will ever read on investments. But it is definitely meant to motivate you to embark on your quest to achieve financial freedom.

The final financial stage of life is when you become an institution or a big-business owner. This is where you employ a large number of employees, and they do the work for you with minimal management required from your side. It is by no means an easy task to accomplish, because it does require you to put in a lot of years of initial hard work, struggle, and risk to achieve this fourth stage of life. A business might have started from a garage, but now it is worth billions of dollars after 30-odd years. It takes an entire lifetime of a single person and then his or her children and future generations reap the rewards. Money starts making money itself, and this is how the rich become richer. Success rates are lower in developing into a big business, and the downside of failing in this stage is that you probably will have to restart from the first stage, making kitchen income, all over again.

The last two stages, investor and institution, are where 90% of the world's wealth can be found. Therefore, it is up to you to decide which stage you want to strive for. You can even do both, since either one will help you get financial freedom in life.

Printed in the United States
by Baker & Taylor Publisher Services